JAMES HOGGARD
NEW AND SELECTED POEMS

James HOGGARD
NEW AND SELECTED POEMS

TCU PRESS
FORT WORTH, TEXAS

TCU TEXAS POET LAUREATE SERIES

Library of Congress Cataloging-in-Publication Data

Hoggard, James.
[Poems. Selections]
New and selected poems / James Hoggard.
    pages cm -- (TCU Texas poets laureate series)
ISBN 978-0-87565-583-3 (alk. paper)
I. Title. II. Series: TCU Texas poets laureate series.
PS3558.O34752A6 2015b
811'.54--dc23
                              2015000789

TCU Press
P.O. Box 298300
Fort Worth, TX 76129
817.257.7822
www.prs.tcu.edu

To order books: 1.800.826.8911

Designed by fusion29
www.fusion29.com

THIS ONE FOR LYNN
AND THE FAST-MOVING STREAMS
WE'VE LISTENED TO

Books by James Hoggard

Fiction

Trotter Ross
Elevator Man: The Bobby Johnson Story
Patterns of Illusion: Stories and a Novella
The Mayor's Daughter

Nonfiction

The Devil's Fingers & Other Personal Essays
Riding the Wind & Other Tales

Poetry

Eyesigns: Poems on Letters & Numbers
The Shaper Poems
Two Gulls, One Hawk: Two Long Poems
Breaking an Indelicate Statue
Medea in Taos
Rain in a Sunlit Sky
Wearing the River
Triangles of Light: The Edward Hopper Poems
Soon After Rain

Translation

The Art of Dying, poems by Oscar Hahn
Love Breaks, poems by Oscar Hahn
Chronicle of My Worst Years, poems by Tino Villanueva
Poems from Cuba: Alone Against the Sea, by Raúl Mesa
Splintered Silences, poems by Greta de León
Stolen Verses and Other Poems, by Oscar Hahn
Ashes In Love, poems by Oscar Hahn

contents

Introduction

James Hoggard, New and Selected Poems, is the ninth volume in the Texas Poet Laureate series published by TCU Press.

With this volume TCU Press continues its honorable task of printing poetry volumes by the Texas Poets Laureate. The most recent publication was a volume by Jan Seale, the 2012 Texas State Poet Laureate. In this volume TCU Press breaks with its established tradition and goes back in time to print the work of a previous Texas Poet Laureate—James Hoggard, the Texas State Poet Laureate for the year 2000.

Reaching into the recent past, TCU could not have chosen a better poet as a starting point. James Hoggard is one of the deans of Texas Letters. Hoggard taught for forty-seven years at Midwestern State University in Wichita Falls, Texas. There he was appointed the Perkins-Prothro Distinguished Professorship of English. In addition to poet, he is a novelist, playwright, short story writer, translator, and essayist. His work has appeared in journals and magazines such as the *Harvard Review*, *Massachusetts Review*, *Ohio Review*, *Southwest Review*, *Partisan Review*, and *Translation Quarterly*. He is the author of more than twenty books. In 1999, he was honored with the Lon Tinkle Award from the Texas Institute of Letters for a lifetime of writing excellence. Hoggard was the recipient of the Hart Crane and Alice Crane Williams Memorial Award for poetry, the Texas Institute of Letters prize for best short story, the Soeurette Diehl Fraser Award for translation (cowinner), the Stanley Walker Memorial Award in Journalism, a National Endowment for the Arts fellowship, and the PEN Southwest Book Award for poetry.

In order to better understand the craft and complexity of Hoggard's work it's helpful to have some background. Hoggard began writing poetry in high school, inspired by Shakespeare, Byron, and Shelley. But he did not limit himself to those classic authors. In his own words:

"During my fourth-year Latin class in high school, as we were working our way through Virgil's 'Aeneid,' I found some rather short poems in an old anthology of poems in Latin and . . . I started trying, as I brought them into English, to see if I could make my translations work as well in English as they appeared to work in Latin."

Then, as if Latin were not enough, he taught himself Spanish so that he could read the work of Octavio Paz in the original language! In college, he also took courses in French and German.

Hoggard considers the primary purpose of poetry to be storytelling and the shaping of voices. That storytelling permeates much of his work, perhaps best illustrated in poems from *Medea in Taos* and *Triangles of Light: The Edward Hopper Poems*.

But it isn't just the narrative and human-driven aspects of Hoggard's poetry that make it so worthy of study. It is also the understanding he exhibits at the sonic level, the very nature of the sounds themselves, which makes all the difference.

In an interview with a reporter from *Texas Monthly*, Hoggard talked about the texture of language:

TM: What do you mean by "muscular rhythms?"

JH: A kind of angularity or hardness, a briskness of tone. For instance, English is a lot less polysyllabic than Spanish and the other romance languages. With fewer syllables expressing ideas, there is an angularity of tone when compared with Spanish. I find it helpful to be reminded of that. I have learned to emphasize or mute the angularity in conjunction with the linguistic spirit and mood of the piece in its original language. So you're talking about much more than getting across literal or idiomatic meaning. You're talking about the texture of language.

For instance, English has a tremendous sense of flexibility that Spanish does not have. Also, English has more muscular rhythms as opposed to that classical fluid quality that the romance languages have.[1]

This characteristic mentioned in this *Texas Monthly* interview—the texture of language, a characteristic of Hoggard's work—transcends boundaries of romanticism, modernism, postmodernism, and so on. This type of attention to language is reminiscent of the Anglo-Saxon/Old English riddle and gnomic poetry. Riddle or gnomic poetry is, fundamentally, a form that provides wisdom to the reader through the use of figurative language (or kennings), usually in the form of a question that readers would have to answer themselves. This type of verse is prevalent among several ancient cultures, but in ancient Anglo-Saxon in particular the use of language is fascinating because of its self-awareness. Riddle or gnomic verse was intended to be read on a sonic level. The lines are full of puns, puzzles, hints, and double meanings; understanding the complexity of the language is absolutely essential to understanding the riddle. Understanding the sounds of language clarifies hidden mysteries. This understanding of the nuance and complexity of language is what Hoggard's work brings.

Out of all the books that Hoggard has written, this volume from TCU Press contains selections from the following:

Breaking An Indelicate Statue
Medea In Taos
Wearing The River
Two Gulls, One Hawk
Triangles Of Light: The Edward Hopper Poems

In addition, there is a generous selection of new poems here.

Texas has played a major role in Hoggard's poetry. Nature and setting have both influenced his southwestern work. The attention paid to those two traits has also informed his other work—which, in turn, has fully fleshed out the characters present in his novels and poems. That is not to say that all his work is about Texas; it certainly is not. It is a contributing factor, though, an environmental absolute that remains part of the fabric of his poetry, explicit or not. Perhaps this is best illustrated by two poems in this collection: "Rattlesnake Hill" and "A Long Winter Run":

Rattlesnake Hill

A rain-gutted sandstone wall
slopes to a brake of brush
where a narrow path winds
toward a light-filled place
in a sunny rocky drop.

Beyond that point bois d'arc boughs
hang so low I have to duck,
side-stepping roots and ruts
as I twist through the overhang.

And now at the edge of the drop,
and alert for what might be in the brush,

I stutter-step into the dry lagoon
then churn up the red clay path.

I might be safe: no rattlesnakes
in sight today—it's been a week,
in fact, since I've seen one.

A Long Winter Run

Molds in the air are burning my eyes
and a stiff cold wind is making them weep,
and I'm running uphill against that wind
to strengthen my legs the flu left weak.

I'll stay out most of the morning
but soon I'll head back into the trees
to wind among dense brushy paths
then into sunlight and the nipping breeze . . .

I'll run this levee till a notion says:
Angle back down to the river road,
follow the asphalt up to the bridge
then turn to go obliquely home.

In the book *Triangles of Light: The Edward Hopper Poems*, Hopper
himself is the narrator. The poems selected from that book for this volume
are exceptional. Consider this excerpt from "Approaching A City":

I know that you and others too
have said the world that I depict
seems God-abandoned, and that all
my lightless portals—empty doorways
and rows of glassless windows—
hum with a damn nostalgia for death,
but that's wrong, most often wrong—
I simply have moods,
and I'm moving toward one now

Everything turns in time toward myth—
What? Sure, I'll talk you through this piece,
and I'll talk you through some others, too

the tunnel's darkness soothes me
and I prefer my windows without glass

. . .

Windows without glass, empty doorways, damn nostalgia. These are connotative images that we can easily associate with all manner of frustrated, angry, disconsolate souls. But that is a combination of the power of Hopper's paintings and Hoggard's words.

The selection of new poems in this volume exhibits another level of Hoggard's poetic skill. The poems are intense, condensed, reminiscent of a Rilke or Neruda. The language is less complex, more contemplative—and powerful in its resonance.

These excerpted lines are from "My Mother Dying":

These days her eyes stay mostly closed and I
sit by her bed and sometimes speak. I hope
I'm doing more than idly waiting for
her death. I do, though, have to say her eyes
seem blind, although at times they turn toward me,
but I have no idea what they might see,
or if they see. I only know I'll squeeze
my mother's hand and kiss her when I leave.

And this new poem, complete:

February In Paris

The pitted streets
we had to cross
were boisterous with noise,
and the snow-melt slush
dirtied the wraps
we walkers wore.

The clarity of the image that suddenly, intimately involves us occurs in the last line. Hoggard helps us own the poem, helps us join into the contract between writer and reader. That "we" becomes not just limited to the pronoun of the invisible couple in the poem. Because of the detail in the previous five lines we, all of us, have become part of the poem. We have walked the streets of Paris.

I have personal favorites among the poems which I can heartily recommend for their skill, beauty, and imagery: "Medea In Taos" (title poem), "Out of Place, Far From Rain," "Breaking the Ice," "Red-tailed Hawk," and "Nighthawks." But I am sure you will find your own favorites. These poems are a master's class in poetry. You will return to them again and again.

Alan Birkelbach
Editor, The TCU Texas Poet Laureate Series

1. Nora Varty, "A Q&A with James Hoggard," *Texas Monthly*, October 2010, http://www.texasmonthy.com/story/qa-james-hoggard.

I
New Poems

A July Mountain Shower

I like the growling, lumbering way
that thunder travels down the canyons here
and how rain takes its slow, good time
in wetting streets, in washing aspen leaves
and mountainsides of fir and spruce.
The air seems freshly fragrant here – it did
a time ago – and although I've no sense of smell,
I still can hear and hearing see
thunder traveling down the mountainside,
a distant avalanche of sound, and metal roofs
being polished red and blue and green.

The rain is falling thickly now,
but no wind blows the rain aslant.
Today no wind blows rain aslant
the way it often does. I've seen
those wildly horizontal blasts of rain,
but now this afternoon the rain
seems soft and long, as if it's settling in,
although I doubt that it will fall this way
for long. These July showers seldom do.

AFTernoon RackeT

I went outside to find a phrase,
but noises there were far too loud
for me to hear a thing but trucks,
their honks and airbrakes screaming
blocks away as sirens pulsed throughout
the neighborhood, the din enough
to frazzle me and scramble speech.

I'd simply come outside to find
a set of sounds to guide me toward
a tale about a world beyond
my own, but noise prevented me
from going where fresh phrases lie,
the racket far too loud, the light
too bright for me to drift toward dreams
that blinding, noisy, wretched day.
I had no way that afternoon
to slide into a shadow world.

So I went back inside the house.
I'd see the world through windowpanes,
through eighty-year-old waving glass
that looked as if a wind had blown
the flatness of the glass awry.
And soon no harsh sounds screamed at me.
The world, my world, seemed silent then
though silence withheld imagery.

DrOUGHT

So go ahead and call this place
the place that gets no rain
because no rain falls here
though memories say rains have
been here – they've swept
through ditches, they've flooded lawns
and drowned roads
so we've had rains,
a lot of rains, and with rain
winds strong enough
to rip ceiling joists loose
and hurl barn roofs away.

A season-SHIFT

The irises mostly gone by now,
sycamores are leafing out,
pecans are dropping their tassels,
bluebonnets are going to seed
and lawns are beginning to green.

Evening breezes are cool
but anvil-topped thunderheads
say high heat is barreling in,
and with it will come big winds
that knock scorched branches down.

February in Paris

The pitted streets
we had to cross
were boisterous with noise,
and the snow-melt slush
dirtied the wraps
we walkers wore.

THE cave

Almost like a breath
a chill moved the air
in the mica-walled cave
I kept returning to.

No moss slicked the ceiling,
no bats hung from ledges,
but the place seemed to breathe –
fool's gold was common there.

ON THE WAY TO RATTLESNAKE HILL

A high sandstone clay wall,
raggedly erosion-slasht,
slopes to a brake of brush
and a narrow path
that winds through shade
to a light-filled place,
a sudden drop onto rocks,
a creekbed that's dry again.

On the way here, and on
the way beyond that point
bois d'arc boughs hang
so low you have to duck
and twist to miss their limbs
and not get snagged by sumac
as you run or mountainbike by.

THE STREAM BELOW ME

Rocks well below the water's rush,
the stream is roiling now,
muddy from the afternoon rain.

I remember how clear it was
this morning when I fished the stream
though no trout struck my flies.

Smoky, the overcast now suggests
more rain might come, and hail,
the dirt in the stream thickening.

This evening there'll be no fishing.
Storms are striking the region,
but breezes soothe our twilight's air.

SIGNS AND WONDERS

Whether they were metaphors, say,
or rare events the few could see,
they did occur, just as the old
hope texts proclaimed they had,

and they still live in good stories,
even in portions of stories,
for fragments often guide us.
Sometimes they're all we have.

And I don't lament that fact.
Sometimes all a singer needs
are a few good notes to take us
into that clarity called song,

though we might end up confused:
head bowed and way off key.

RUNNING ANOTHER KIND OF HILL

I know how hard today's wind blew.
To run against it was to run
against a driving wall, a wall
that barreled toward you fast, a wall
that threatened to undo your legs,
but then you made another turn
and harsh wind's power died – your legs
turned loose again, your legs turned light.
You did not have to heave to breathe.
Your legs were stretching comfortably.
You thought you might be good to run
like this all day so next block up
you turned then turned again a block
away to head again against
the wind. That works as well as hills
to help your legs stay in fine shape.
The kind of wind that we have here
can be transformed to hills most days.

MY MOTHER DYING

Although I know what loss is near, what loss
will come when Mother leaves, when Mother dies,
I will not talk about another world,
a world that's better, say, than where she is.
The fact or absence of that world is not
what drives me now, for I know what I'll face —
deep loss, slow separation from the one
who with my father let me know, when I
was just a child, their love was fully mine,
no matter what I did or what I said.

But now she's weak and cannot speak, and yet
somehow she has a lovely look, her skin
so clear and smooth, her features fine, the way
they've always been. No grimace pulls her lips
or cheek aslant, the way I'd heard they'd been
when morning dawned and nurses' aides
came in her room intending to prepare
her for the day but found she'd had a hard
downturn and could not speak or eat or drink.

These days her eyes stay mostly closed and I
sit by her bed and sometimes speak. I hope
I'm doing more than idly waiting for
her death. I do, though, have to say her eyes
seem blind, although at times they turn toward me,
but I have no idea what they might see,
or if they see. I only know I'll squeeze
my mother's hand and kiss her when I leave.

II
Poems from *Breaking an Indelicate Statue* (1986)

Breaking An Indelicate Statue

Our nontouch lust chisels the shapes
of all that I am talking of,
but I feel more than lust. I have
for you a rough deepshadowed love, just now confessed.
Mosaic law forbids it, but not my peace of mind,
for conscience is but shadow of a rock.

Times times times I've gone by where you sleep
and felt the bodypull of brainlove
that grows enormous in the length
of all that you are: distance that falls like stone,
static that sparks alive the hem on your thighs
where your razor has never yet shaved.

There is more than one stopping point
we strain against in making light our heavy fight
against the bounds in which our motions go.
There is clothing and prudence of speech,
eyes that flash then dilate in restraint,
like matchflames frozen by a wild heatpromise,

and hands that keep to themselves
pretty much of damnably all the time,
and words too judicious to grab your shoulders—so
the hairlines above your knees
are only one stopping point, but I keep hacking north
of that line to your soul—brainlusting

for the rhythms of our skin and its wild yet articulate speech.

SONG OF REBECCA CALCUTTA

R.C.
b. 1871 – d. 1908
We did not know her
R.I.P.

My country is a myth and a swamp.
Men are paddling their canoes tonight
in the moonlight dance of lilypad bulbs
sleeping over quicksand.

I love these men rowing in my swamp,
these handsome shadows of the will-o-
the-wisp, eternal like my candles
and vague, vague like my heart.

My country's grown rich with water and plants
whose roots have never pierced rock,
is wild with shivering fish.

But many feet down I know there are rocks
where the bones of snakes have lain,
where the caverns of wind are too dark
to see the rocks that have killed.

The murder of light makes dusk of day.
Songs of the swamp are too old
to be sung by the trees' agony,
and the myth that devours is mine.

My land is a raft nailed by birdbeaks
and lashed with petrified ferns, and I
am large like the cypress trees, humble
like the sun that has gone.

And I am large like the cypress trees
and humble like the sun that has gone.
I am bitter like the taste of snakeskin
and long like the years

pulled toward the light by the power of doom.

GETTING GROCERIES

Passing by the produce
I notice how terribly soft
the avocados are

        Once in a car

The cart's wheels sigh
along the linoleum floor

        we lay beneath
        a stardrunk sky
        Clouds came, and rain

The frost on orange juice cans
glues my hands
to iceburned tin

        Your eyes and arms
        have sometimes been
        a flood upon me

Marking my load,
the register snickers at me
then gobbles my check

        and my fingers
        have disappeared in your hair

I should've gone ahead
and bought the damn avocados

ELPENOR IN HELL

I keep asking myself, Was it worth it?
To go crazed that night on a drunk
for the hot and anonymous touch
of two thighs I became pig to,
and to pass out then on the roof
unmindful in my greenness
of the ecstasy in the seasoned glory of starlit sky
or a woman I'd fight Poseidon
to get home to.

But idiotlegged and rank
I woke to my older friends' clamor
and tumbled off the edge—

and the bulge of my neck-knot now tells me
the frenzy was sham.
Broken, my body is monstrous.
Though my rheumy eyes gush wild with fog
shadows are all I ever saw.

Unlike Achilles who also sobs,
I made no choice. I drifted,
lost in what's called youthful fashion
whose frenzy, Tiresias now tells me,
lacks the core of earthcentered passion.

PaTriotism

Little lovely fatbaby jumpered
in green, supine
with her froglegs hanging
off the couched toter,
Buddhabeautiful in sleep,
my daughter who starts
at a chairscrape
then slides back in soft sleep
while her sweetly raging laughshouting brother,
my son, tickles her toes
in his awakedream.
I would kisshug them both
if I had less respect
for the privacy of their play.

Partial Reunion

If I hadn't've known
you were doped up
I'd've said you were crazy,
which you are.
Floating through the toys
and douche kits and stationery
in your beige nylon gown
to the prescription counter,
you looked like Ophelia
two months out of period.
You'd had the staph infection
scraped from your head.
There were other demons, though,
they didn't excise—
your mother for one
who would've been shocked
to see you in public
in bedclothes.
But I wasn't shocked.
I kept eating my hamburger
and thinking how crazy you looked
with puffy eyes and hungover hair
and was glad you blindly passed by
because what the hell
is there to say
to an ex-wife
who nurses on acid
from her widowed mother's imaginary breasts.

GETTING MY SOURCES STRAIGHT

Reading serious stuff, I
noticed her noiselessly begging
to share her little book

and smelling the sweet
wetness of babyshit, I
brought her up in my lap.

We read our things until
she wanted down and slid off of me.
Doughy stuff cookied my pantsleg.

While I cleaned us, she kept
as quiet as her stories
of lost toy sailboats

and now she's bunched asleep
in clean diaper and gown,
a curl of silent angel's mischief.

Offertory

Shortly after supper we
were greeted by our neighbors
with four dead ducks,
bloodywinged and bubblymouthed teals.

They were happy with their kill,
and while we were talking they
folded the heads under wings and
jammed together the bills

into violently horny frenchkisses.

I agreed to come over soon
to play pingpong, and my wife
remarked that we'd enjoyed
the fish they'd brought two weeks before.

While they talked about the taste
of crappie and roast duck,
I watched the speckled down
mounding plumply, healthy breasts

receptive to a molding and venal touch.

Fullfisted with ducknecks,
they gloriously mumblesang
of marksmanship and the scads
they'd blast to hell come morning.

The ducks, roughly handled icons
of lust, malleable in death,
seemed serene, as if life
in its tension were awkward

and death in its limpness had effortless grace.

III
Poems from *Medea in Taos* (1999)

MISS KATIE

She had these hands, gnarled hands,
the knuckles themselves like fists:
knots set in a row,
bruised coffee-colored knots

and we whispered about her,
whispered lots,
but all the hush in our voices did
was smoke our eyes and purse our lips,

thin bitter lips,
and twist the tendons in our necks,
but most of us kept muttering,
muttered lots,

terror growing in us like mold:
we were frightened
scared we were growing our own
twists of bruise-colored bone,

ours, though, hiding inside us,
lodged away from sight,
invisible without an x-ray
or exploratory knife

RIPOSTe

with Borges in Orono

So that evening in Maine he got me back
We'd been talking about the Argentine
my father having given some sermons there

"Ah yes," he said: "God—I worked him
into a story once, but you do know
he's better in English than Spanish
Most poetic things are—Spanish is stiff,
far too formal for talk about God"

But when, he asked, had my father been in B.A.,
and as I told him he said that he
was about to leave then for the States,
then smiling at me he added there were only two things
one had to know to know politics then:
"Eva Peron: la puta, y Juan: el cabrón,"

and watching him twisting his hands down into his lap,
I was thinking of jesters and fools
teaching the delight that comes when connections break
"A lot you do," I said, "parallels that"

"What do you mean by fool?" he asked,
glancing sharply at me
                              "Clowns," I said,
but he insisted I explain,
so I brought in Jung, flashed notes he'd made
on tricksters and dreams in Navajo lore

"I don't know Jung, I never read Jung,"
so I referred him to Yeats, to *A Vision*,
to the Fool as child of God, but he snapped,

"I don't like Yeats—you don't, do you?"
"Why not?" I asked
                              "Nasty," he said,
"a mean little nasty man"

Though I wanted remarks on the Fool,
the nimble little cripple dancing near God,
he insisted he knew nothing
about anything like that,
then someone whispered in my ear,
"He's stringing you on, Jim—he'll do that—
in fact two weeks ago he gave some talks
on exactly what you're getting at"

Glancing back now, I smiled
at the smirk being sent my way
He'd been right to nick me back
Earlier in the evening I'd been
the only one on the program who
never mentioned the frail
little blind man's glorious name

HOW TO MAKE COQ AU VIN

First wash the chicken—birds and people
have touched it before you,
you don't know where they've been.

Now section the flesh, lay the pieces
in a pot—I prefer a narrow one—
juices do best when they rise high,
and you want the soak to go deep,
as far up into the meat as it can.

Now quarter three onions and slide them
down in the pot with circles of carrots
and bite-sized chunks of potato.

Next add a cup and a half of wine—
Burgundy's best—you want your meat
ripe-bodied and sharp—
most often that's what you want.

I needn't prescribe the condiments here,
the amounts of garlic and salt to use,
or pepper and basil and thyme—
spices are a lot like love—

so cook the mix slowly, at not much more
than a simmer—the mix needs to steep,
needs to be in heat all day.

Think of yourself with someone you love,
think of you both in bed all day,
the wrap and the press of your flesh
blushing your skin with its heat.
By night you'll be ready to eat.

Anniversary Trip

It was not evil, though it looked that way,
the copperhead wrapped round a branch
four feet from our eyes by the Brazos,
a river once called Arms of God.

After beaching our canoe for lunch
we had lain on a slope on the bank
then moved to a clearing for shade

where a breeze, sliding coolly now
through our loosened clothes,
fingered its way across us,

a salt cedar brake and scrub oak mott
screening us from public view.

Letting skin see in its own oblique way,
I let my gaze drift, but my breath
disappeared, my eyes now locked
on an oddly long knot

twisted on a branch twisted before us,
and the dark ragged bands were not wood,
and the shotlike red eyes did not blink.

Look straight ahead, I said, *don't move.*

And fingernails now biting blood
from our palms, we rose,
and the brush seemed to watch us
as slowly we moved away

in a way we have not always done,
memory saying we'd see that snake
everywhere we looked the rest of the day.

THE CHINESE BRIDGE

across the Tigris in Mosul, Iraq

The Chinese built the bridge, and one
of them, legend says, is buried beneath it.
He was down in a hole adjusting a form
to set a pillar in when someone tripped
a switch and a load of quick-drying cement
poured down like God's wrath on him.

Some say, however, such never happened.
No one reports hearing moans near there
at night when lost ghosts cry, and no one
going through the eucalyptus forest nearby
reports seeing will-o-the-wisp flares,
the hearts of sad souls catching fire.

Maybe so, that may be, the agreeable say:
Perhaps the body's not there, never was.
But it is, others insist, it is there,
and the absence of sign is truth,
for the absence of an outcry after death
is the surest sign of the fact of death.

OIL FIELD ROAD OFF CLYTE ESCARPMENT

Ground squirrels dart among
the prickly pear, larks
warbling morning in as hawks
ride rising waves of heat,
and on the split-topped ridge
yuccas prong the slate-blue sky.

Like a shadowed vision of dust,
a coyote loping across the road
disappears in mesquite brush,
and I wonder: When will it break
hard into a run, to roll a rabbit,
rip open its stomach and lungs?

Past noon the heat's a weight
whose whipping winds feel
like catclaw cuts, and our legs,
turned heavy, want to drop.
Halfway blind, you're dizzy,
the world's so full of mirages.

Then night, when it comes,
if it comes, settles in
with a moon-washed breeze,
and the scorched clay cools,
and a rattlesnake glides
toward a mouse in a ditch,

but with eyes in its hair
the mouse bounds off,
its black-tipped white tail
guiding its kangaroo leaps
toward a shadow, the slit
between two sandstone thighs,
but the rattler slides inside there, too.

Medea in Taos

No, the next morning she did not wake
to horror. *I didn't even go to bed,*
she said: *I was distracted but the fits*
didn't start till later. I must admit,
of course, I just knew her old, back when
she lived near here for several years.
Both noon and night she haunted La Fonda
and we'd often walk off time together.
Neither ragpicker nor rich, she always wore
a short-crowned, wide-brimmed green hat aslant
her brow to keep the sun's glare off her eyes
and hide the wrinkles that webbed her face.
But ghosts of beauty still lived wild in her,
made her recall the nights, those lyrically long
sweet-sweating nights, when Jason came down,
like a golden god, she said, upon her. *O how*
he thrilled me then, she said, *and he was good,*
too, strong and loving before he went nuts
for that coy young tart: the little bitch
built hipless like a boy, with useless breasts
barely bigger than bumps. O I made sure no power
on earth would sing sunbursts within that womb.

When she spoke like that, madness, I learned,
was rising to slap her, and I could do nothing
to help her. But whether I left her alone
or not, she'd come tearing hard at me
with curses and fists and, swarming me, swear
she'd never collapse: *I'll never go limp again—*
never! I'll rage till my tongue scorches rock,
she said as veins ticked across her temples
and, swelling, stitched seams down her neck.
Scorpions! she cried: *They're fighting to death,*
they're fighting deep in me—their stingers!
My God! she cried: *This pain won't stop*

till I learn how to sing—I don't know how—
I sling chaos, chaos slings me. When I pass
by children at play or asleep I curse them—
they shriek and my curses catch fire, their skin
begins sizzling, I stand there entranced,
I stand near the flames and watching them burn
I watch without shame.

Then one morning she was gone and never came back,
and no one I know ever discovered where she went,
but even now sometimes during wind-bothered nights
when the moon hangs gibbous and a lone puma screams
near the top of Iron Mesa, memory shouts at me:
I did, I did see her, I'm sure of it, from the side,
last week, studying leeks at market. I passed
by her twice. No, not then, not last week,
I saw her last month, in Veracruz, on the street—
no, not her, not there, but in Zacatecas last year.
I have seen her, though, and I still see her.
Her eyes, like a hawk's talons flexed for snakes,
come at me cold and dun and sharp, crazed
with spleen and grief. *And all those mad wild cats,*
she says, that wail out there, like tortured ghosts,
that prowl out there where lava lies, are dreams
of mine, and all the children I set on fire are me.

THE MATRIX

Norway, late tenth century

Around my neck a stone emblem
that looks like a cross.
It's a short-handled hammer,
a circular shield
       holding Thor's sign:

an amulet not for luck,
for force: a spur to spur
the upraised fist
       slashing through wind,

an image of Christ
       resurrected in rage,
an icon of Thor:
       his extension of hand
       splitting the overcast sky.

I hear in the sign a cry
waving off a blood-scabbed slab.
What I see, though, is still,
dark redness in me
locked deep in my chest.

I am the hammer
and the stream I look through,
and I am the cross.
My own deranged image
       bounces back at my eyes
       but my vision holds only a ghost
       framed in an oval of oaks.

Salvation, I am learning,
here in this grove,
is only a word
but words I have learned
are flesh and wood

Salvation, I think, is a wish
and illusion a condition of life.

ADMONISHMENT

Listening to the news tonight
I thought of Virginia Woolf
walking into the river to drown.

Her long horseface,
sensitive to tremors
lyrical voices sing with,
floated in with the waves,
but we never heard bonebreakage
coming from her implosion
or the bursting rip of lungs

nor did we hear
Triton absolving her breasts
from suckling the fish.

A war is going to occur
and our dream of escape is dead.

Tonight we wait for a message
from the land where Jesus died.
Waiting, we shrink from the world
and some of us hold our breaths
while hearing seawaters lap.
Our legs and arms grow tired,
our voices weak, our muscles sore.

On a day like this Virginia Woolf
walked into a river to drown,
to submerge herself in a region
whose underdrafts are ice.

THE DYING GAUL

Museo di Capitolo, Rome

With his eyes downward lost on the marble
which when he died
did not exist in this shaped form:
was raw in the hills
with rabbits and wolves
he parabolas the firm and alien earth

the dyed clay pomading stiff
his now wild hair
his torque an omega
his length an ellipse
a broken sword
useless before him

and a wound in his side
where Christ's would be

His runner's legs scan a silence
that booted heelclicks fill
and always he is dying
though the end of his breath
lasts forever

EMILY'S GIFT

Even if she were as reclusive
as some of the legends say,
and I doubt she was,
though I do like the notion
bright light crazed her eyes,
she wedged a phrase in us

that makes us name her
when we notice that light,
drifting into our rooms
like sequences of thought
that give our flesh fact, slants.

She gave us the phrase
but keeps taking it back.
That light-slant, she snaps,
it's mine, I named it,
and of course she's right,

but Lord, she has an edge—
I've heard her cry her claim
all over the world,
but the time I remember best
was a March afternoon in Spain.

At 3 p.m. in Seville the sun
ran a beam through a notch
in the wild cathedral's side,
and the light-bar kept rising
up a dark stone slab

dividing the altar's back
from the ambulatory,
but the organist would not play
till that slanting shaft

lit Jesus himself crucified
in the glory of the light

beamed on the gray stone wall.

OUT OF PLACE, FAR FROM RAIN

In three weeks the rainy season begins
in San Miguel where I wish we were
strolling the narrow cobblestone streets.
Sunday night, we would have soaked all day
at Taboada's hot springs and had
rounds of tacos mixtos and beer
at Rodriguez's café then pastries
at the Basque bakery on Calle Dolores.
The promenade would have begun.
Taxis would be trolling the plaza
and I would still be debating buying
a machete to bring back here
for assaulting sunflower stalks,
johnsongrass and nettles. I wish
it would rain. I wish a lightning storm
would blow the lights so candle flames
might glow in the breeze swimming
around the creaking leather chairs
we'd be sitting in while talking about
rhythms of fire in the dancing Greek past,
our toes munching cool tile floor
and our breaths as sweet as papaya.

VIGIL and SLEEP

You look so distant now,
except in memory where we speak

and though I know you're just asleep
I also know that death
will end this sleep,

and laying my palm across your wrist,
I notice the planes
that shape your head
seem like gestures of ageless grace,

then stroking the breadth of your brow,
I lower my eyes
and again am moved by a fact of flesh:

the intelligent look of your hands,
your mouth locked open for breath.

IV
Poems from *Wearing the River* (2005)

Breaking the Ice

We'd gone to where trotlines were.
We hadn't set them but we checked them,
and when we found good fish
we cooked them near our lean-to,
then finding the long vines that hung
off the cottonwoods near the river's bend
we grabbed them and swung out
over the deep pool as far as we could
then dropped into the clay-red drink where,
the winter before, ice broke beneath me—
the freeze not as hard as I'd thought:
I'd wanted to see if I could ski across the Wichita,
but my breath quickly gone, I was flailing,
splashing through shards and mush,
but the ice wouldn't hold, and panicking,
I kept lunging, trying to stomach my way
onto a sheet of uncracked ice.

First I was desperate, then pissed.
I smashed my fists down, breaking the ice
that was biting my chest, and clubbing it
time and again, I sloshed my way out
onto rime-whitened mud then pulled
myself free with salt cedar shrubs.

But days like that were years ago
when wilderness seemed new, when
nearing home in the cold, we'd hear
the ghostly hum of the power lines
that spanned the canyon where,
when spring came, we had firecracker fights.

Running, we'd hurl our lit explosives,
of course, at each other: smoke and noise
celebrative things, for we were young then,

children who set our traps near riverbanks—
we had plans to be furriers soon, and our traps
were close to where the ice broke beneath me
where, thrilled, I lost my breath
in the splash of a chin-high chill.

Louisiana Dawn

Couplers clanging on a slow freight train,
I had to wait before crossing the tracks
on my way downhill to the riverpath
I had never run before, the ghostly dawn dense,
I could scarcely see the slapping waves
or sodden straw that trashed the winding bank,
and only the peaks of a long suspension bridge
floated above the ectoplasmic hardwood trees
in a forest where snakes slept the winter away,
and the world disappeared in a pewter sky
that was hanging as low as the brush that day,
the rot between trees already mulch,
and the noise of the lurching train
was assaulting the dawn awake.

SKIING THE BAYOU

Before I jumped from the boat to slalom through
the wide lagoon to the wave-crazed lake—
wind high that day, sky threatening walls of rain—
Matt said, as I put my ski on and fixed my line:
"Be careful of the cypress stumps, and if
you see a gator, don't panic, or fall,
just keep in mind, in spite of their size, they're shy,
and keep your lane away from the banks:
banks are where the snake nests are,
though cypress stumps are worse:
hit one of those you disturb the snakes,
but first you'll likely find
a stump's found home between your eyes."

Ranch Walk

Clicks began coming from the brush
where we'd gone to pick berries
but the off-beat rhythm was weak
and the clicking soon stopped.
Don't think so, I said, and agreeing
it wasn't a snake, we moved on
through a tangle of sumac vines
to find volunteer blackberries,
but the crop was pitifully small,
and the wild tomatoes, what few
there were, having been bitten,
had rotted, so we turned to wind
back to the pickup, but again
I stopped, saying, *Wait*, pointed
down where, a few feet away,
a five-foot-long rattler
was sliding parallel to us,
having come from the brush
near where the berries were,
and now we knew why the buzz
had sounded erratic and odd:
only one rattle hung on the tip
of its blunt black and white tail.

WHen even one IS HIT

When even one is hit the world explodes,
the mystics have kept telling us,
and though some will reject grace
hot rain, if rain should come, will bathe us.

The mystics have kept telling us
despair will be the fate that's ours
unless hot rain, if rain should come, bathes us
and scalds a scabrous portion of our world.

Despair will be the fate that's ours,
and we won't change that fact unless
we scald a scabrous portion of our world
to foster justice and redemption now.

And we can't change our fate unless
we learn to think and act clearly now,
to foster justice and redemption now
in compensation for the blood we've lost.

But trying to think and act clearly now
we know that some will reject grace
in compensation for the blood we've lost.
When even one is hit the world explodes.

RED-TAILED HAWK

Its feathers ruffed by the fierce north wind,
the hawk stayed fast on its live oak perch

then, as if releasing its breath in its wings,
it rose, slowly rose, and finding the right current,

sped from the leafy mott and would not return
till talons and beak had been washed in blood.

correcting plato

1

I like to think
that God's first word
was thunder,

a celebrative
explosion of noise
echoing off
newly made matter,

as if thunder itself
were a comment
on the lightning flash
that caused it.

2

That first thunder,
like all thunders since,
came from the force
that stirs speech,

and the drama
of the voice
is the meaning
of the voice,

God from the first
being partial to things.

when the Deer Ran the Peaks

The rain came in but no wind blew,
for a time the wind stayed gone,
but when wind came the sleet came too
and the wind stayed the whole night long,

and no moon rose through the storm
and no moon shone through the gloom,
and full of fright the deer ran off,
and full of fright and swift in flight

they sped through the brush they ran
to a cold fast stream, and there
took drink, ears perked, they shied,
fell back to boughs while night lay black

then the fierce wind died, sky cleared,
stars rolled, but the air stayed cold,
and dreams that danced in the deer
turned wild and shook their flanks,

and frost smoked out of their mouths
like ghosts as they rose with the sun,
but all day sleet lay slick on clay,
and sharp, their hooves crunched ice

and wind stirred cold, but the deer
ran the slope, and high, a plain
broke the rise, and swift once more,
the herd ran past the last trees' line,

ran in the clear, ran past a rock spring,
scratched hides on rock their hooves
clicked on, and the air they gasped at
thinned, but still they ran, they rushed

up slopes then sped down slopes, they ran
toward the sun, toward the sun's white light,
sun's heat the source of spring and rain,
they ran till deep dark fell—they ran!

ENGLISH WIT

She didn't swing, she whipped
her small black purse
as she sashayed toward the Thames
in her leopardskin faux-fur sheath
and leopard-spotted ankle socks,
her shoes stiletto-heeled.
She was walking her black toy dog,
pulling it behind her on a leash.

Then not long after that
in a trimly cut three-buttoned suit
a derbied gentleman strutted by
jauntily clicking his walking cane,
and he had a toy dog too.
His, though, had fallen,
but still in harness, the little beast
skidded behind him on its side.

RaTTLesnake HILL

A rain-gutted sandstone wall
slopes to a brake of brush
where a narrow path winds
toward a light-filled place
in a sunny rocky drop.

Beyond that point bois d'arc boughs
hang so low I have to duck,
side-stepping roots and ruts
as I twist through the overhang.

And now at the edge of the drop,
and alert for what might be in the brush,
I stutter-step into the dry lagoon
then churn up the red clay path.

I might be safe: no rattlesnakes
in sight today—it's been a week,
in fact, since I've seen one.

A LONG WINTER RUN

Molds in the air are burning my eyes
and a stiff cold wind is making them weep,
and I'm running uphill against that wind
to strengthen my legs the flu left weak.

I'll stay out most of the morning
but soon I'll head back into the trees
to wind among dense brushy paths
then into sunlight and the nipping breeze.

I'll run this levee till a notion says:
Angle back down to the river road,
follow the asphalt up to the bridge
then turn to go obliquely home.

DOme anD FauceT

There's an ancient mosque in Mosul whose dome
looks as if hair is growing on the dome.

High winds have lodged enough dirt there
that weeds and grass sprout on the dome.

A suq and water faucet with a glass on it
are near the mosque with the balding dome.

But recently bombs exploded near there.
Did their shocks wreck that headlike dome?

And if the voices the mosque houses are mute,
are dust and stone all that's left of the dome?

The people I saw drink from the public faucet
put the glass back—it looked like a dome.

V

Poems from *Two Gulls, One Hawk* (1983)

1

Get right to it, a near voice said:
Say it straight

    No way, I said:
    Crooked's better

Say Being is a tree
whose top twigs touch
the lower reach of heaven

    And be thought a fool?
    Hell, you
    do some listening awhile

    Then the first one said:

Tree and truth share a root

    But the second replied:

Not any more

Tree and true were the same
From treow came treowth
and from them troth

    Commitment, not Being—
    thrashing is what the tree is

Keep going. Say:
Fidelity's the force
reaching upward
beyond wetness
into light's source

    It stretches downward too

Into inward-turning folds
of earth's moist darkness:
the womanpart of world

That's what I said. So
let gusty breezes
be pageantry and sing:

> Love is the thirst for the eternal
> and earth the desert
> we stay hungry in

I wince at such bromidic truth

> And I smile at how quotable
> the strong sensations of illusions are

There is in breath, in passion
which gives breath speed—

> Stop!

Yes? he said, listing

> Speed!

Sped at first meant prosperity

> Sped meant power

The two were the same
There is, he said, continuing:
There is in passionate breath
an arm thrown round the knees
of the immortal

Desire appears quickly

Its reception is a seawaving through
the changes of animal breath

    Inhaling & exhaling,
    no matter if fast
    no matter if slow —

As long as a glimmer or murmur of the immortal appears

    Breathing is not dependent on that
    and unity does not last
    in the flesh or in the mind
    The chaos out becomes the chaos in

Unity is a seawaving through troughs and crests

    My desire for its presence,
    its stillness of presence,
    twists me into pain
    When I go into the pit of myself
    I mess up my life

The undulant waves rise and fall
through the rhythms pushing blood
The intimacy you're cast off from comes,
returns when you receive the desire
to be at one with one

    Bring that booger on

Earth and sky join in a grove
A crowd gathers round

    Leave the many in their mobs,
    turning inward in their mobs,

I want no part of the alien self

Intimacy, as you call it,
goes inward too
That force called lust erupts—

It once meant plainly desire

That force called lust gives blindness sight
The hell with the many
I'm craving connection with one

That force called lust erupts . . .

For out from under feet
grasshoppers sprayed like omens
but their sounds were dry,
a pulmonary clicking,
bones being rapped in the woods:
the martyrs were learning new games,
and I was once a martyr
sucking at the pit of self
messing up my life

Reflection and reason—

Piss on them both

Long ago, in the time before we were,
elders and youth worshiped ancestors

In dance, in prayer, in play
We've lost the raunch in rite
The chaos out: the chaos in

They lit fires whose piquant smoke rose
toward celestial homes

The earthly ones were too damn confusing
The young ones rattled the house

The smoke I say rose

    circling above the lower boles
    before disappearing past the leaves
    into illusion –

Into the sun
which burned marsh dankness
into fragrant mist

    Self's swamp still stinks,
    no matter how wistful you get

This time, you're right, we cannot do the same
We cannot honor ancestors
in the style the old ones used
Ancestors now are only shapes,
names stamped in books by machines

    The old ones, hell, were always names
    Latter-day folklore made them more

The illusion, its truth, made them more

    Don't drone another muttered mass
    The energy of the old ones is useless

Unless we remember them in prayer

    Unless we accept the tensions they bring

But, as you in strain say: Lust erupts

    Winds chap faces

The winds never rest
at the point of imbalance
where we just were
and are again
this moment and the next:
burned to leather on the plains

But when Being—

Damn you. Listen!
Seawater laps. New beaches form
far away from here except in mind
Fields await our walks

With indifference you think

With vengeance more likely

Only if you maim them

By god, you're more animistic than I thought

Sounds of grasshoppers return

The wind
cool on sweating neck
comes back

like a song's clear melody

singing up out of the wreckage of lust

Or do you mean dust?

The words rising from us
fall back in new shapes

I hear a rustle in the leaves
Is it a serpent?

      Snake, you prig

Or is it a friend?
Or neither one?

      A whistling comes now too

and the image of a lean-to,
the sight of a deer at dawn

      A fawn or a faun?

My eyes, my eyes! They're burning!

    2

For a time I wondered why
St. Teresa said she preferred
the monotony of daily labor
to the ecstasies of vision

      Soon I knew
      the greatest wonder lay
      not in her insight
      but in our urge
      to commemorate strong sensation

      Our milder responses, she teaches us,
      are perhaps more memorial
      than we ever thought
      We forget them

We ignored what she said

for there is a thrill
in the maniacal
and another kind of thrill
in cool and lasting peace

      Sombitch, the third one said:
      stillness don't exist
      Even your saint knew that
      Of course, she had no kids
      House apes we used to call them
      when we were giving our own parents fits

You're breaking the spell

    There is no spell

      Live with a kid in a harried time,
      try to do something witty
      like entertain a vision or two
      and more than a spell will break

You must, though, try to sustain
the precious desire for clarity

      Live with a kid
      in the weather on the plains
      and precious desire becomes bald urge

For what?

    A flash of connection with one's mate

But there is no stillness

So get on with your truth,
climb that tree you were moaning about

    or break a couple of bottles
    and fight, it's time we broke
    ourselves some skull

The wind today promised
to blow rain here
The sky darkened
but no rain fell
Heat's weight
kept descending upon us
The dog days were coming

    dog days were already here

        and I howled in my heart
        but my mouth released no sound

    3

    For a time after watering my garden
    I sat in a hammock
    watching my son and our dog
    playing tug-o-war with a sock

    My sense of connection with them
    was stronger than my invention
    of doing the same thing

for I was never a child
who played with his dog
while his father watched

and I, unlike my son,
never had to leave one parent
to live with another

> Hell, you never even had the chance

The drama is not in me, I confess
The drama is somewhere else
I am a fulcrum
Extremes slide toward me
when the stirring winds are right—
I'm sinking into the pit

Perhaps you were never as happy
as he seemed that day

Perhaps your father
never took his fatigue
to a hammock

> He was workin' his butt off
> He didn't hunker down like you

The past seems like something others had

When you adopt it as your own
you alter it for pleasure,
you alter it for effect

> The past does not exist

except as a whimsy of now

or an ache

or an image which allows you to lie about . . .

 St. Teresa received me into her bosom
 Neither one of us knew what to do
 though we had a mild laugh
 and I helped her sweep the place clean
 She thanked me for it
 then took a dose
 of silence again

   She never was known
   for being much of a barfighter,
   was she? I think not

4

 Somewhere in me, prior to blood, antecedent to mind,
 in the neural portion of what I am
 time blows storms all through me

Dust rushes through trees
Limbs scratch roofs
A horse goes wild with fear
Clouds scud
A funnel comes down: sky's augering whorl

  an image of extension:
  heaven touching earth
  mayhem mayhem mayhem

   Just blowin' it all to hell:

The forming of a new shape
caught in the moment of explosion
before the new shape has a story to tell

I am not this night telling stories
I'm listening to my son chatter with my wife
His windy talk wears both of us down
I am not even waiting for a story to form

nor am I telling the truth

Tomorrow morning I shall not go out I think

Lust turns sour when locked in mind's caves

There is too much distraction tonight:
my son chanting, "Santa's coming! Santa's coming!"
out of season
as he brings in the kitten
in a pillowcase
and drops it on the floor
along with a load of chatter
he piles upon the desk

How can I descend into the coals of ancient fires?
How can I do anything but drink myself to sleep?
The distractions are exposing how vacant I am

You're fighting the vagrant self
Your son's more interesting than
a celibate, broom-wielding nun

Earlier tonight I saw the moon
A cross was flowing from it
but I couldn't remember
what the sign meant

All day I'd felt gut-sick,
bitter that my flesh
was only worth sticks —
I craved an odalisque

Or St. Teresa?

The cross reminded me
of someone spread-eagled
Clouds soon came
and covered her up, or the moon

You were only fighting self
for no good purpose

Your dog was panting
and so were you,
and I wasn't far from being out of breath myself

How can I descend now into ancient fire?
How can I do anything but drink myself to sleep
and rue the fact that St. Teresa's mind
is (or was?) more evenly paced than mine

VI
Poems from *Triangles of Light:*
The Edward Hopper Poems (2009)

Approaching a City
(EH on his 1946 oil)

Whether you have in mind talk
or other intrusive atmosphere
I'll remind you: movement and sound
often bother me—chatter's offensive
and I don't like the habit many have
of interrupting good spreads of light
If they'd ditch their shadow before me,
but not their mass, I'd be pleased

I know that you and others too
have said the world that I depict
seems God-abandoned, and that all
my lightless portals—empty doorways
and rows of glassless windows—
hum with a damn nostalgia for death,
but that's wrong, most often wrong—
I simply have moods,
and I'm moving toward one now

Everything turns in time toward myth—
What? Sure, I'll talk you through this piece,
and I'll talk you through some others, too
the tunnel's darkness soothes me
and I prefer my windows without glass
There are 58 of them here, and not
a one's involved with grief or God

It was Sunday, simply Sunday morning
and I, in the memory I've depicted,
was coming back home on the train
I'd been awake all night,
and glad the goddamn trip was done,

I liked the fact no nuisances were out:
neither racket nor motion nor people:
just a tunnel, my entrance home,
a tunnel to lead me smoothly home

NIGHT IN THE PARK
(EH on his 1921 etching)

Of course, I placed him there,
the man at the end of a bench,
his back's forward roll curving him
into the paper he's reading
in a pool of spilling light,
the bulb barely in view above him

and the blur of foliage
fanned around him
is at least as visible as he is,
and as important as he is,
shadow and light being life to me

And as he reads I notice that
his knees and feet triangulate
the pond of light he's sitting in:
the shape of light conveyed
in much the way that darkness is,
as passive space,
the void between the stars:
a terror to some,
but pleasure to me

NIGHTHaWKS
(EH on his 1942 oil)

They are not human, except in disguise
A hatchet-faced crew, their eyes
are sockets of darkness that catch no light

Forward-curving, their backs make them seem
as if they're perching on limbs
in a windless world where light, spilling out

from their aerie, triangulates all
the planes it touches: sidewalks
and streets, open windows, and wedge-lit walks

NIGHT ON THE EL TRAIN
(EH on his 1918 etching)

What finally depressed them,
both of them literate
was how clichéd their passion was:

the meeting in secret,
the banal vocabulary lovers use,
their unwillingness to junk

inconvenient mates—
I watched them and I saw
how when doubts crept in

they'd try to worry doubt away
Leaning together they'd try to believe
they were more than clichés

sun in an EMPTY ROOM
(EH on his 1963 oil)

No, hell no, I was not
meditating on death
or notions of emptiness
I meant what I presented:
unadorned slabs of light
on two unaddled walls,

but when you asked
what I was looking for
in peopleless planes,
I said, Myself—what else?
for light is where self is
if self itself ever is

Neither misery nor peace
finds voice or home here
though a window does
and with it a blur of leaves,
salves for a claustrophobe
There's nothing abstract here,

and nothing metaphorical,
and except for several ghosts
of gridmarks I've left
all planes are walls or floor,
and chiaroscuro is flesh,
and shadows, stains to mark
where light finds speech

MOONLIGHT Interior

(EH on his 1921-23 oil)

I only remember moments now,
my brush the mnemonic device
through which I discover
and sometimes even invent
events of a fragmentary past

The brevity of it all still an ache,
she seems like a glance in a dream
whose textures are blurred,
but her auburn hair is loose,
like the moon-white curtain's gasp,

and the gable across the way
is an eye in tension with mine,
but I no longer see
the woman's face—
she's stepping away from me,

but as she does I see
the moon's soft light
sliding down the length of her back

SKYLIGHTS

(EH on his 1926 watercolor)

I do see the world triangularly
and there have often been times
that finely tight shape
moved past me to my paint,
as it did with this roofscape,
the building I had my studio in

The crunch of the scene attracted me:
the mortar smears on brick façades,
the vent pipe thrusts
and steep roofslopes,
and the narrow passageways
groined between them,

and an overcast sky that's limitless—
wedge after wedge of planes,
and abandonments of light
the hopeful call shadows—
but I call self

OFFICE aT NIGHT
(EH on his 1940 oil)

I'm not that man
working at the desk —
he's a guy I invented,
and the woman turning toward him
is not ogling him,
she's simply someone
who'd like to skinny out
of her clinging clothes,
and the man, though he looks
like me except for his hair,
has lost himself in an invoice

The shade swells
at the woman's glance,
as if the guy subliminally knows —
no, she's the one who knows
the power of flesh
cannot be contained
by file or desk or chain

ROOM IN BROOKLYN
(EH on his 1932 oil)

The light, passing by a vase,
seems to stop at her feet
but she's not the focal point
This is room and cityscape,
inside scene and outside scene,

and the room's the way I like it,
spacious and tastefully spare,
and if there are people about
outside, I can't see them there

No one mars my city's line,
and the woman with back to me
is a shadow-dimmed form,
not a voice interrupting me

SUNLIGHT in a cafeteria
(EH on his 1958 oil)

I can draw figures
and light on walls
but not always the face
whose facile gestures
sometimes bother me

More to the point
is the fact I've cut
urban bustle out,
and the two I've left
are sitting alone
in a large room
where a vast flood of light
overwhelms the place,

the way one in France
who read me Verlaine
once overwhelmed me

Her face ceramic
as if it's a mask,
the young woman reads
her fingers and palms
while the youth
pretends to study
the brown flaring leaves
of the window plant

This dream keeps returning:
she's everywhere:
the blue of her dress
is in the chairs,
in the flowerpot's rim
and across the street

on the bottom step

Painting them, I paint
us all – I paint us
into symmetry,
the speech I know:

light a transient thing
entering this room,
overwhelming this room,

the way one in France
who read me Verlaine
once overwhelmed me

summer EVENING
(EH on his 1947 oil)

The porch tonight belongs to them
and the light they're in fortifies them,
and young, they've learned to speak
with a comfort I don't have,
and only a few I know have had

No anger bleeds on them tonight,
and though there's tension in them
no demons made them wooden-limbed
the way my figures have sometimes been
Somehow I quickly got them right

Leaning back against the balustrade,
her body brave with sensual speech,
she seems to be comfortable with
the kiss of light down all her length

The young man, though, is trigger-tight,
as I would be if she were mine,
though no junebugs or other pests
slap wall or door or face this time

Acknowledgments

My mother wrote in my baby book that I liked to make up stories, but the indication was that she was pretty indifferent about whether she had in mind lying or a nobler kind of creativity. I'll likely never know what her interpretation settled on. Was I a miscreant, or was I artful? As classically appreciative of the arts as my family was, it makes sense that my parents were not especially interested in the works of a neophyte. And odd as it might seem, that was fine with me. And lively and gifted as she might have seemed, my master works English teacher also seemed, shall we say, reserved about what I was trying to accomplish. She did not appreciate the fact that some six weeks my literary interests focused more on my own work than on the grand masters we were supposed to be studying. I have to admit, though, that I appreciated her admonishments. Only a fool would have thought that with or without aid I had reached high levels of literary achievement. There were walls of off-putting people out there; but there were gate openers, too, I trusted. But who were they? And where would I find them? And when? Then the truth struck me. I had already met some of them. They were almost everyone I had met or would ever come to meet.

ABOUT THE AUTHOR

Because his phrasing seems so easily eloquent, so in tune with his themes, James Hoggard has often appeared to be a wizard of form. A two-term president of the Texas Institute of Letters—a rarity in itself—he has published more than twenty books and won numerous awards for his writing, including the Lon Tinkle Award for excellence sustained throughout a career. He was also recently named a Fellow of the TIL, the highest award the prestigious organization can give.

Hoggard's work has appeared widely throughout the United States in such journals as *Southwest Review*, *Harvard Review*, *Partisan Review*, *Translation Review*, *Chelsea*, *Manoa*, and *Mantis* (Stanford); he has also given readings and lectures in Cuba, Mexico, England, France, Spain, and Iraq. He recently retired as Perkins-Prothro Distinguished Professor of English at Midwestern State University, where he taught for forty-seven years.